Images of
Cape Breton

Images of Cape Breton

Photography by
Warren Gordon

Foreword by
Silver Donald Cameron

Steel Town Publishing

To my mother and father

With special thanks to Sherman Hines, Master of Photography, without whose friendship and guidance I would have neither this book nor my career in photography.

Canadian Cataloguing in Publication Data

Gordon, Warren 1951-

ISBN 0-9690395-0-6

1. Cape Breton Island, N.S. — Description
and travel — Views. 1. Title

FC 2343·4·G67   917·16'9'0022   C80-094539-5
F1039·C2G67
Second Printing

Foreword

Cape Breton is a magical republic miraculously washed ashore to adorn and ornament an otherwise unsalted nation. Cape Breton is a large island, a small community, a depressed region, a tourist's shimmering memory. Cape Breton is an astonishingly complete and satisfying environment, a sovereign state of the mind.

How can this be? Cape Breton is, after all, only the smaller part of a small province. It has fewer people than suburban Mississauga, Ontario. (A dozen years ago, government economists were chirping that the island would have lost half its population by the mid-seventies. It didn't. Cape Bretoners are tenacious, and they love their home.) It is a working man's island — a land of farmers and fishermen, of papermakers and steelworkers and coal miners. It is a place of taverns and bingo games, of Woolco and the village store rather than Saks and Bonwit Teller.

If one knows where to look, Cape Breton also harbours world-famous authors and film-makers, authorities on Louis XV furniture, celebrated yachtsmen, potters, weavers, painters, and photographers. What other community of this size speaks four languages on a daily basis — French, English, MicMac and Gaelic? Cape Breton was the most important of the MicMac Indian domains, the site of the Indians' great summer celebrations. The MicMacs have been supplemented by enough Scots to make Cape Breton the heartland of Scottish culture in America and by enough Acadians left over from the Bourbon empire to make two large areas of the island overwhelmingly French.

Its musical culture is particularly vital. Traditional fiddlers play with rock bands, coal miners' choruses headline the pop festivals, performers convert the airs of Inverness County into a fresh musical style for television. Many of the verses in this book are the work of local songwriters, indeed, and song seems perhaps the most indigenous of all Cape Breton's arts.

Music, history, folklore, painting, radical politics, fishing, sailing, tragic and uproarious stories — what excites you? You'll probably find it in one of Cape Breton's many faces. And yet, under all the many works of men and women on the island lies the stark and seductive reality of the land and the sea, the mountains and islets, of the secret waterfalls and boiling tideraces, the leagues of forest and the heaving, restless ocean. Bitter and desolate in winter, in summer lush and sensuous, Cape Breton is at once awesome and intimate, a landscape of infinite surprises and challenges. Cape Bretoners are wedded to their island environment as the flame is wedded to the candle.

This, I think, is why Warren Gordon has compiled such a contemplative, silent selection of photographs. He photographs the Sydney Civic Centre, not from the clotted traffic of the Esplanade by day, but from the quiet stillness of the waterfront by night, with a huge, motionless moon poised in silver amusement above it. The building is impressive, a bold statement of faith in the city's uncertain future. But it is surrounded and surmounted by realities which will outlast it, however long it remains in place.

This dimension of the Cape Breton viewpoint is surprisingly little understood. The hard-drinking, fighting, dancing, striking Cape Bretoner is an accepted archetype of Maritime mythology. His romantic and religious side is less familiar: the meditative figure sitting on the beach as the dawn rises out of the gilded ocean and the terns and herons prowl the shallows. The dance is over; the fever has subsided; it is time to think of ultimate things.

To understand that calm, reflective undercurrent in the Cape Breton outlook, look at the island as Warren Gordon sees it. Warren has his sense of humour — consider the photograph of the goats in this collection — but the images he captures are not of the bustle and roar of work and play; they are of motionless fishing boats, empty roads, solitary houses. Warren's photos echo with lonely, private chords. They offer a long perspective behind our daily frets and worries.

Still, the photographs are not all privacy and solitude. A person stands behind them, and his name is Warren Gordon. We are viewing the images which are important to Warren. Hushed and spectacular, these are the images, he thinks we can use.

What is Cape Breton, anyway? A good place to shed the plastic nonsense and random noise which bedevil us and to contemplate ultimate matters: struggle, loss, beauty, love, pain. Cape Breton is a good place to wrestle with failure, emptiness, and death. After one has come to terms with these massive darknesses, perhaps one is at last ready to value the light, to live with joy and grace and appetite, to make pictures, to make books, to make music, to make love.

The true record, writes the Cape Breton poet Joseph MacLeod, is not of books
>but found
>in the body
>of the man
>of the land.*

That is the record which Warren Gordon seeks and seeks to share.

Silver Donald Cameron

Cleaning the Bones. Erin, Ontario: Press Poreepic, 1977.

Marion Bridge

Out on the Mira on warm afternoons,
Old men go fishin' with black line and spoons,
And if they catch nothing they never complain,
I wish I was with them again — — —

Can you imagine a piece of the universe
More fit for princes and kings?
I'll trade you ten of your cities for Marion Bridge
And the pleasure it brings.

Out on the Mira the people are kind —
They treat you to homebrew, and help you unwind
And if you come broken, they'll see that you mend,
I wish I was with them again.

Now I'll conclude with a wish you go well —
Sweet be your dreams, and your happiness swell.
I'll leave you here, for my journey begins.
I'm going to be with them again.
I'm going to be with them again.

Allister MacGillivary

Marion Bridge

Christmas Island

Margaree Harbour

Mabou Harbour

S̀ e Ceap Breatainn tir mo ghraidh,
  Tir nan craobh, s̀ nan beanntan ard́;
S̀ e Ceap Breatainn tir mo ghraidh,
  Tir is aillidh leinn air thalamh.

My Cape Breton is a fine land,
Land of trees and mountains tall.
My Cape Breton is a fine land.
Land of beauty dearest of all.

Dan Alec MacDonald

Pierce Peters, Fiddler

Cape Rouge

Come all ye hearty truck drivers and listen to my tale,
And you will know the reason why I'm sitting in this jail.
I drove a truck, I loved my work, I was a mighty driver.
Let me introduce myself — John Alex Hugh Mac Ivor.

I said I was a mighty driver, well I proved it on the day
I put Whitney Pier, Whycocomagh, and Cheticamp away.
I thought of my poor family and I knew I could not stop
Till Inverness was in the cab with Arichat tied on top.

Driver MacIvor, when will I be set free?
Locked up in a jailhouse for moving old C.B.
C.B. to them meant radio, to me it meant Cape Breton.
I put the island in my truck — now twenty years I'm gettin'.

Ronald MacEachern

St. Margaret of Scotland Church, 1841
River Denys Mountain

And more especially do we thank thee, O Lord,
For the gut of Canso, Thine own body of water,
Which separates us from the wickedness
That lieth on the other side thereof.

"Favourite prayer of a Cape Breton
Presbyterian minister in the 19th century."

Canso Causeway

Gabarus

Driftwood is burning bright.
Wild walk the wall shadows.
Night winds go riding by,
  Riding by the lochie meadows.
On to the ring of day
Flows Mira stream singing.
Caidil gu lò, laddie, lò laddie,
Sleep the night away.

Kenneth Leslie

Mira River

Corney Brook

Neil's Harbour

Bras d'Or Lakes

Arichat

Gabarus

Daddy is on the bay,
He'll keep the pot brewin',
Save all from tumblin' down,
Tumblin' down to rack and ruin.
Pray Mary send him home,
Safe from the foam singing,
Caidil gu lò, laddie, lò laddie,
Sleep the night away.

Kenneth Leslie

The Point, Ingonish

Low Point Light

Bay St. Lawrence

Sail, sail the coast to the one you love the most,
And a seaman hates to boast but my heart's larger
For a girl named Jenny Lou
With the giant eyes of blue
And I'm thinking of you in Neil's Harbour.

Sam Moon

Off Neil's Harbour

Alexander Graham Bell Museum, Baddeck

"I have travelled around the world. I have seen the Canadian and American Rockies, the Andes, the Alps, and the Highlands of Scotland, but for simple beauty, Cape Breton outrivals them all."

Alexander Graham Bell

Margaree

Christmas Island

Each night in a dream
Cape Breton I see,
Where the mountains and valleys
Spill mist on the sea,
And the music is calling
Through sunlight its song
While the farmer is waking
The sky up for dawn.

Oh, it's sweet as the heather
And rough as red wine,
Where the music runs fiddles
And pipes through my spine.

Dennis Ryan

Mabou

Kelly's Mountain

Middle River

And it's oh, Caitriana
Bear me upon your wing.
Fly me to the Highlands
Where heaven's birds sing.

There's a song there upon the wind
Where the ocean meets the sky,
Soundin' like my father's violin
As he gently played a lullabye.

Kenzie MacNeil

Cabot Trail

Lone Shieling

Tarbot Vale

Mary Ann Falls

Ingonish Ferry

Seal Island Light

Gillis Lake

McAdams Lake

Winter winds were wildly blowin',
White were the fields and skies from snowin',
Poundin' as hard as the heart that's knowin'
When it's going home . . . .

Kenzie MacNeil

St. George's Church, Sydney

Mira Road

St. Ann's Bay

When the world's up in arms
And they're paving the farms
And you can't find the peace that you've known,
It's like a play that you're in.
Let the next act begin.
Every mile takes you closer to home.

Leon Dubinsky

Ingonish

Fourchu

Fourchu

Green Cove

Ducking the spray,
They go sailing away,
Red faces straight into the wind.
They're dripping and shifting,
Oh boy, how they're lifting,
It's off to the Banks they will go.

Haul away, the whole long day,
Bearing the toil and strain,
Restless and free, you're part of the sea,
Fathers of children like me.

Fred Lavery

Elmer MacGillivary
Fisherman, Fourchu

South Bar

Bras d'Or Lakes

Now I'd been told throughout my life
To leave and look for more,
But what more could I ever have
Than a life on Loch Bras d'Or?

Kenzie MacNeil

Seal Island Light

Bluenose II, Sydney Harbour

Sailing ships upon the ocean,
Wood and wind and water,
Glorious days and glorious notions
Were wood and wind and water

Forests of masts stood in the harbour.
Proud were the men of the trade,
And the hopes ran high in the Maritime sky
For fortunes were there to be made.

Oh, whatever became of the bountiful sea
And wind and water.
Gone, gone so mysteriously
Are wood and wind and water.

Kenzie MacNeil

Roger Muise
Fisherman, Cheticamp

Main à Dieu

They go down with their nets to the shore.
They go down like their fathers before,
And the sea seems to say, ''If you ride me today,
I will grant you the wealth of my store.''

They are sea people, the pride of the land,
Strong of the spirit and rough of the hand.
Sea people the waters command
From their rocky old steeds of the strand.

Allister MacGillivary

Wellington Rafuse, 79
Active Fisherman, Fourchu

Irish Vale

For these island threads are fine but strong
No matter how far away you may be,
For they let us to laugh in the sun
And to love by the moonlit sea.

Kenzie MacNeil

Gabarus

Gabarus

Capstick

In Isle Madame and Arichat,
They always put out the welcome mat,
''Mais oui'', ''bonjour'' is where it's at,
Along the shores of Cape Breton.

Where the heart is strong and the hand is rough,
Where times are usually always tough,
Where enough is always more than enough,
Along the shores of Cape Breton.

Max MacDonald

Cabot Trail

Eskasoni

Micmac Dance Troop

"Even today, the Micmac refer to themselves
as Onamag* people of Cape Breton."

Rev. D. MacPherson
Onamagee is the Micmac name for Cape Breton Island.

Lingan Mine

There is danger lurking on every side,
In the deep, dark land of coal,
Where no ray of sun ever finds its way,
And above the seas may roll.
With a cheery smile on his grimy face,
He emerges from that black trap
That fearless man from the deeps below,
The man with a torch in his cap.

Helen MacDonald

The Late Fabian Young
#26 Colliery, Glace Bay

Heavy Water Plant, Glace Bay

Sysco at Night

Pouring Molten Steel

Filling Ingot Molds

Over the rooftops and over the trees,
Within these new townships, oh what do I see?
I see the black pitheads, the coal wheels are turning,
The smoke stacks are belching and the blast furnace burning,

And the sweat on the back is no joy to behold
In the heat of the steel plant or mining the coal,
And the foreign owned companies force us to fight
For our survival and for our rights.

Kenzie MacNeil

Blair Oake
Sysco Steelworker

St. Mary's Church, East Bay

Fortress Louisbourg

Along Cape Breton's coast line/stark and grey and tall
Stands a living legend/and a wall.
She's the Fortress Louisbourg/famous in her day,
Called the second Dunkirk/but today . . .

She stands alone, facing the sea,
Who knows what pictures stain her memories!
She was queen, she was mistress, she was pageantry —
She was tragedy.

Allister MacGillivary

Sentry at Fortress Louisbourg

Kitchen Worker at Fortress Louisbourg

Louisbourg Harbour

Angie Aucoin, Spinner, Middle River

Holy Rosary Church, Westmount

Mira River

When the sunlight dies in the western skies
With a violet-red farewell,
And the firefly glows in the lilac rows,
And cricket choirs swell,

If you see it stream, this poet's dream,
And in praise your silence keep,
You will catch my own sweet island home
As she takes her highland sleep.

Allister MacGillivary

Sunset Reflections, Sydney Civic Centre

Tarbot Vale

Over an ocean and over a sea,
Beyond these great waters, oh what do I see?
I see the great mountains climb from the coastline,
The hills of Cape Breton, this new home of mine.

We come from the countries all over the world
To hack at the forests, to plough the lands down.
Fishermen, farmers and sailors all come
To clear for the future this pioneer ground.

Kenzie MacNeil

Sunrise Valley

Great Bras d' Or Channel

We are an island,
A rock in the stream.
We are a people as proud as there's been.
In soft summer breeze or in wild winter wind,
The home of our hearts: Cape Breton.

Kenzie MacNeil

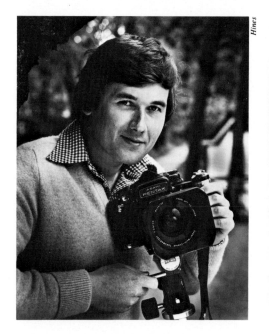 

Hines

Warren Gordon's roots in Cape Breton go back to the eighteenth century, when an ancestor on his mother's side was granted lands including much of what is now the North End of Sydney. His father's family, meanwhile, landed in Pictou, Nova Scotia, and made their way to Cape Breton in an open boat.

Warren Gordon was educated at Sydney Academy, Xavier Junior College and St. Francis Xavier University. After graduation, he worked with Sherman Hines, Master of Photography and creator of such well-known books as *Nova Scotia, Outhouses of the East*, and, most recently, *Atlantic Canada*.

Since 1973, Warren Gordon has operated Gordon Photographic Limited, a major photographic studio in downtown Sydney, and has received regional and national recognition for his work, including the awarding of the degree of Craftsman of Photographic Arts.

In 1985, Mr. Gordon mounted a photographic exhibition at the request of the Highland Regional Council of Scotland. This exhibition toured throughout the Highlands and Islands of Scotland to inform the Scots about Cape Breton and its Celtic Heritage.

Mr. Gordon's second book, "Cape Breton: Island of Islands", was published in 1985 and has received an enthusiastic response.

Silver Donald Cameron

Silver Donald Cameron grew up in British Columbia, and lived in California, England, Halifax and Fredericton before settling in D'Escousse, Cape Breton, in 1971. His radio plays, television scripts and award-winning magazine articles have made him one of Canada's best-known writers. He is the author of five books, the most recent being the best-selling novel *Dragon Lady*.

Verses arranged throughout the book are excerpts from complete works by some very talented writers.

Song for the Mira, Sea People, Louisbourg, She Takes Her Highland Sleep *Allister MacGillivary, Cabot Trail Music*
Cape Breton Lullabye *Kenneth Leslie*
Ś e Ceap Breatainn *Dan Alec MacDonald*
Driver MacIvor *Ronnie MacEachern*
Girls of Neil's Harbour *Sam Moon*
Cape Breton Dream *Dennis Ryan, Fogo Music*
Caitriana, Winter Winds, Loch Bras d'Or, Wood, Wind, and Water, Island Threads, The Island *Kenzie MacNeil*
Man With The Torch in his Cap *Helen MacDonald, Waterloo Music*
Every Mile *Leon Dubinsky, Shagrock Music*
Along the Shores of Cape Breton *Max MacDonald*
Fisherman's Song *Fred Lavery*

All photographs were created using Hasselblad and Pentax 6X7 equipment and Vericolor and Ektachrome film.

Vericolor film processed and printed by Pro Color Lab, Halifax.

Ektachrome film processed by Maritime Color Lab, Dartmouth.

Design
Dennis Page Graphic Design

Design Assistance
Andrea MacIvor

Project Co-ordinator
Stephen MacDonald

Assistants
William K. Hollohan, Albert McArthur, Louise Gillis, Jacqui Corbet, Dawn Monahan

Many thanks to the people who contributed to the creation of this book.

Kenzie MacNeil, Max and Colleen MacDonald, Ralph Dillon, Ron Caplan, Shirley Hines, Norman MacDonald, Barry Nagey, Brian and Valerie MacDonald, Pierce Peters, Kay MacDonald, Jim Lorway, the MacAulays of Inverary Inn, Sarah Denny, Bill McKee, Terry MacLellan, Tom Tighe, Gordon Purves, Ray Martheleur, Lorne Rogers, Dave Devison, Bill Gouthro, Elmer MacGillivary, Mike and Marcel Crimp, Kleran Ballah, Andrea MacIvor, Fr. Brian MacDonald, Norman Noiles, Elizabeth Boardmore, Stu Killen, Theresa Young, Phil Murphy, Herb MacIntosh, Robert Morgan and Silver Donald Cameron for his excellent introduction.

We wish to acknowledge the cooperation of the College of Cape Breton Press and its director, Stephen MacDonald.

Printed by
Everbest Printing Co. Ltd., Hong Kong

Gordon Photographic Ltd.
Steel Town Publishing
367 Charlotte St.
Sydney, N.S.
B1P 1E1